# THE TRUTH ABOUT LOVE

## FACT, SUPERSTITION, MERRIMENT & MYTH

THE TRUTH ABOUT LOVE

PHILIP ARDAGH

# FACT, SUPERSTITION, MERRIMENT & MYTH

Illustrated by Marian Hill

MACMILLAN CHILDREN'S BOOKS

First published 2001 by Macmillan Children's Books

This edition published 2013 by Macmillan Children's Books
a division of Pan Macmillan Limited
20 New Wharf Road, London N1 9RR
Basingstoke and Oxford
Associated companies throughout the world
www.panmacmillan.com

ISBN 978-1-4472-0784-9

Text copyright © Philip Ardagh 2001
Illustrations copyright © Marian Hill 2001

1 3 5 7 9 8 6 4 2

A CIP catalogue record for this book is available from the British Library.

Printed and bound by CPI Group (UK) Ltd, Croydon CR0 4YY

*For the love of my life, of course!*

*It is impossible to love and to be wise.*

From 'Of Love'
– Francis Bacon (1561–1626)

# Contents

# Cupid

CUPID IS THE Roman god of love, *cupido* being 'love' or 'desire' in Latin, the language of the Romans. He's often identified with the ancient Greek god Eros. (The Romans often stole, renamed and worshipped Greek gods.) Unlike Eros, who looks more grown-up, Cupid is a beautiful (and often slightly chubby) winged boy, blindfolded and carrying his bow, with a quiver full of arrows on his back. According to myth, if one of Cupid's arrows hits you, you instantly fall in love.

But why the blindfold? To illustrate that love is blind, that's why. You can't choose who you fall in love with. It just happens, like a bolt from the blue . . . or like an arrow from Cupid's bow.

According to some, Cupid has two types of arrow: gold and lead. If you're struck by one of his golden arrows, your love is pure and virtuous.

If you're struck by one made from lead, your so-called love is more about passion and pleasure.

*I swear to thee by Cupid's strongest bow:*
*By his best arrow with the golden head.*

From *A Midsummer Night's Dream*
– William Shakespeare (1564–1616)

# The Heart

WHY, OF ALL the internal organs, do we traditionally love with our heart? Perhaps it's because the heart often beats faster when we're in the presence of the one we love, or pounds away in our chest. It's simple to see how, over time, it would become associated with that loving feeling.

Obviously, different cultures have different beliefs, but images of the heart representing love date all the way back to ancient Egypt and became particularly popular on Victorian Valentine's Day cards. The arrow one often sees drawn through the heart – representing both the sudden way in which love can 'attack you' and the fact that love can be a painful process too – is supposed to have been fired by Cupid.

*Two souls with but a single thought,*
*Two hearts that beat as one.*

From *Der Sohn der Wildnis*
– Friedrich Halm (1806–1871)

# Love and Marriage

IN MANY CULTURES and in many cases, love results in marriage. Another word for marriage is 'wedlock' and there are plenty of jokes about the word having something to do with being 'locked into' – trapped in – marriage.

In truth, the word comes from two Old English words: *wed* (meaning a pledge) and *lac* (meaning action), so 'wedlock' is actively taking a pledge to show commitment and (hopefully) love.

## Tying the knot

Getting married is often referred to as 'tying the knot', which relates to the binding nature of the wedding contract. In some traditions, there is literally a knot-tying element to the wedding ceremony. In the Hindu marriage ceremony, for example, the groom knots a ribbon around the bride's neck. Traditionally, before the moment the knot is tied, the father of the bride can refuse to allow his daughter to marry and the ceremony is halted. Once the knot is tied, however, no one can stop the marriage.

## Taking the man's name

Often – though certainly not always – when a couple get married, the wife gives up her own surname and takes the surname of her husband.

So if, for example, an Octavia Smith marries a Julius Jones, she becomes Octavia Jones. This tradition is a variation on a Roman one: on marrying, the bride would be described as being 'of' her husband . . . in other words, belonging to him. So Octavia

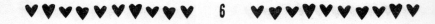

would have become 'Octavia of Julius'.

This probably wouldn't go down quite so well today!

## Something old . . .

Numerous superstitions have sprung up around weddings and the marriage ceremony. One of the more familiar ones concerns what the bride should wear, though its exact origins are uncertain. It's remembered in a rhyme:

*Something old; something new;*
*Something borrowed; something blue.*

## The wedding cake

It's said to be good luck to keep the top tier of a wedding cake for the christening celebrations of the newly-weds' first child.

Of more interest to the unmarried guests, however, is putting a piece of the wedding cake under their pillow that night. This is supposed to make them dream of their future spouse (but often ends with little more than a piece of squashed cake).

Some variations on this ritual require you

to borrow the bride's wedding ring, which probably wouldn't be too popular.

## Catching the bouquet

Apart from the groom not seeing the bride until the marriage ceremony on their wedding day, one of the best-known superstitions concerning weddings often results in plenty of pushing and shoving and whoops of delight.

It's the one which says that the woman who catches the bride's bouquet of flowers – when she turns around and throws it high over her shoulder – will be the next one to marry. This was originally an American custom, probably based on the much earlier eighteenth-century custom of the guests throwing stockings at the bride and groom *in bed*.

*[Marriage] resembles a pair of shears,*
*so joined that they cannot be separated;*
*often moving in opposite directions, yet*
*always punishing anyone who comes*
*between them.*

Quoted in *Lady S. Holland's Memoir* (1855)
– Sydney Smith (1771–1845)

# The Wedding Ring

THE WEDDING RING is usually made from gold and worn on the 'ring finger' – the one next to the little finger – of the left hand.

Why gold? Because it has always been considered a pure, beautiful and valuable metal, so it's ideal for representing something as important as marriage.

Why that particular finger? Because the ancient Egyptians believed that a special 'vein of blood', or nerve, runs from the ring finger of the left hand to the heart, which is the seat of love within the body.

## The Holy Trinity

In the Roman Catholic wedding ceremony, the thumb and next two fingers represent the Holy Trinity of Father, Son and Holy Spirit and each of these fingers is touched with the wedding ring before the word 'Amen' is spoken and the wedding band slipped on the ring finger.

## Switching hands

Wedding rings haven't always been worn on the left hand in Britain. It wasn't really until the 1700s that Protestants stopped wearing them on their right hands, with Catholics switching even later than that. In some countries, wedding rings are still worn on the right hand.

## Worn with love

Few truly antique wedding rings remain today, because most Victorian and pre-Victorian wedding rings were made of twenty-four-carat gold. The purity of gold is measured in units called 'carats', twenty-four-carat gold being the purest there is. ♥➤

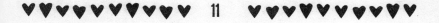

## THE TRUTH ABOUT LOVE

Pure gold is a very soft metal and, if worn as a ring on a finger, wears away over the years. Eighteen-carat or nine-carat rings – made of gold mixed with a harder metal – may not be as valuable as pure gold rings, but do last longer and can be passed down.

*Pussy said to the Owl, 'You elegant fowl!*
*    How charmingly sweet you sing!*
*O let us be married! too long we have tarried:*
*    But what shall we do for a ring?'*

From 'The Owl and the Pussy-Cat'
– Edward Lear (1812–1888)

# Rings on Their Fingers

AS WELL AS wedding and, of course, engagement rings, there are other types of ring closely associated with love. The ring is said to be an endless or eternal loop, symbolizing eternal love . . . which also, conveniently enough, fits on a finger!

The most common of these are the Claddagh ring, the gimbal ring, the true-love-knot ring and the eternity ring.

## From the Emerald Isle

The Claddagh ring is made of gold and usually contains no gems. It is moulded in the form of two hands holding a crowned heart and the design is originally supposed to have come from a town called Claddagh in Ireland. The crown is said to represent loyalty, the hands friendship and the heart love.

If the ring is worn with the bottom of the heart facing downwards, towards the hand, it means that the wearer has a sweetheart and is 'taken'. If the bottom of the heart points up towards the fingertip, then he or she is available. And note the 'he or she' part: both men and women commonly wear Claddagh rings.

## When two become one

The gimbal ring also goes by the name 'gimmal' or 'jimmal' ring, but they're all one and the same, and the name is derived from the Latin *geminus*, which has nothing to do with gems but means 'twin'.

This metal ring can be worn as one by one person, or split in two and worn by two:

ideal for lovers. The two halves of gimbal rings are usually wavy so that they can intertwine, fitting together tightly, rather like a puzzle.

## Tied together in love

The true-love-knot ring is just that: a ring with a knot in it, denoting true love, often made of gold or silver. There are numerous variations on this design. Some such rings are designed to look as though they're made from tiny pieces of rope or string. As with Claddagh and gimbal rings, these can be worn by men and women, though more commonly by the latter.

## For ever and ever

Eternity rings have the jewels set in the band (rather than in a cluster, as with an ordinary ring) and, in the case of a full eternity ring, the jewels run all the way around the ring. More common now are half-eternity rings where, as the name suggests, the jewels go halfway around.

## Say it with stones

In Victorian England, there was a craze for giving the woman you loved a ring which spelled out a message of love with the first letter of each precious stone set within it. Two of the most popular messages were 'DEAREST' and 'REGARDS', thus:

| | |
|---|---|
| **D**iamond | **R**uby |
| **E**merald | **E**merald |
| **A**methyst | **G**arnet |
| **R**uby | **A**methyst |
| **E**merald | **R**uby |
| **S**apphire | **D**iamond |
| **T**opaz | **S**apphire |

Names were often spelled out the same way. Rose, for example, was spelled out with ruby, opal, sapphire and emerald. Some names were much easier than others and if you were lucky enough to have a 'd' in your name, it meant you'd be sure of getting a diamond in your ring.

## A girl's best friend

Speaking of diamonds, why do engagement rings traditionally contain them? The answer lies partly in their beauty and partly in their rarity. Diamonds used to be very hard to come by and, therefore, very expensive. To give your loved one a rare, beautiful and expensive ring was the ultimate sign of your affection; a sentiment that still survives today.

# Wedding Anniversaries

WHAT BOOK ABOUT love would be complete without listing the traditional types of gift that one is supposed give married couples on particular wedding anniversaries? (Not that they might thank you for some of them nowadays.) The idea is that the longer a couple has been together the more valuable the tokens of love should be. The origins of these gifts (or, more accurately, the materials from which they should be made) are somewhat blurred, but

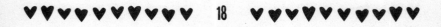

you can rest assured the Victorians played their part.

As with so many traditions and rituals, versions do vary.

| | |
|------|------|
| 1st: | paper |
| 2nd: | cotton |
| 3rd: | leather |
| 4th: | fruit/flowers |
| 5th: | wood |
| 6th: | iron |
| 7th: | wool/copper |
| 8th: | bronze |
| 9th: | pottery |
| 10th: | tin |
| 11th: | steel |
| 12th: | silk |
| 13th: | lace |
| 14th: | ivory |
| 15th: | crystal |
| 20th: | china |
| 25th: | silver |
| 30th: | pearl |
| 35th: | coral |
| 40th: | ruby |
| 45th: | sapphire |
| 50th: | gold |

55th:    emerald
60th or 75th: diamond

Queen Victoria celebrated her 'Diamond Jubilee' after sixty years on the throne so, as a result, the sixtieth wedding anniversary became the time to give diamonds instead of at the more traditional – and very unusual – celebration of seventy-five years' marriage.

Today, the wedding anniversaries most commonly celebrated in this way are those from twenty-five years onward, and are referred to by the type of gift which should be given. For example, a celebration of fifty years' marriage will be referred to as a 'Golden Wedding Anniversary'.

*In spite of all romantic poets sing,*
*This gold, my dearest, is an useful thing.*

From 'Mira to Octavia'
– Mary Leapor (1722–1746)

# Goddesses of Love

IN GREEK MYTHOLOGY the goddess of love was Aphrodite (pronounced *Afro-dye-tee*) and in Roman mythology she was Venus, but they were both one and the same, simply going by different names. As I said earlier, the Romans had a habit of appropriating all things Greek, including their gods. (See Cupid on page 1.) The ancient Egyptians had Hathor (who, in turn, had originally been worshipped by the Nubians) and the Vikings had Freya.

## Aphrodite and Venus

Aphrodite was born in the sea. She's shown emerging, naked, from a huge shell in a very famous painting of her (as Venus) by Botticelli in the fifteenth century, which is now reproduced on everything from wrapping paper to mouse mats. She may look all sweetness and light, but Aphrodite/ Venus not only had plenty of love affairs, she is also famous for her foul temper. She's staring straight at us in that painting, not looking demurely away.

## From cat to cow

Hathor was originally a goddess of war from Nubia who took the form of a vicious lioness, but, on becoming the ancient Egyptian goddess of love and childbirth, she became a friendly-looking cow at the same time. In fact, her milk became the food and drink of the gods. But don't be fooled. She was one of the most powerful and important among them.

## From the frozen north

As the Norse goddess of love and desire, Freya sometimes flew around in a hawk-feather cloak, sometimes rode around on the back of a huge boar and sometimes travelled around in a chariot pulled by cats! She also found time to lead the Valkyries, the warrior maidens who carried dead battle heroes to Valhalla, the hall of the slain.

Like all these love goddesses she was very beautiful (by the standards of those who worshipped her) and was, to use a modern phrase, one tough cookie.

*She fair, divinely fair, fit love for gods.*

From *Paradise Lost*
– John Milton (1608–1674)

# Pheromones

THERE ARE SOME people who claim that falling in love has more to do with chemicals than anything else; the spoilsports! Many animals (and some plants) produce chemical signals called pheromones. These are odours (smells) which can mean anything from 'This is my territory, so stay away!' to 'I'd make a great mate, so why not come up and see me some time?'

It's pheromones that often make an adult's sweat smell, something which doesn't happen with young children.

Different types of animals use pheromones

in different ways, and that includes insects. We now know that pheromones play a part in the behaviour of primates too, and humans are primates.

Just how much these chemical odours influence our behaviour when it comes to being attracted to someone, though, we just don't know.

If you have a partner, do you think he or she smells great? Does that have to do with their aftershave or perfume . . . or is it something far more primeval than that?

*Drinking when we are not thirsty and making love all year round, madam; that is all there is to distinguish us from other animals.*

From *Le Mariage de Figaro*
– Pierre-Augustin Caron de Beaumarchais
(1732–1799)

# Prune Stones

PRUNES – DRIED PLUMS – have never been a favourite with children. This is hardly surprising, what with their wrinkled, leathery skins, strange-tasting, syrupy juice and large stone at their centres. But it's these stones that offer a bowl of prunes and custard some redemption.

It was claimed that, if a girl put her prune stones on the rim of her plate and counted them up once she'd finished eating, it would reveal the profession (or lack of one) of the man she was to marry. (In this enlightened age, women can have the selfsame professions, so this can as easily apply to a prune-eating boy too.)

The number of stones and their meanings are:

1. Tinker
2. Tailor
3. Soldier
4. Sailor
5. Rich man
6. Poor man
7. Beggar man
8. Thief

This would suggest that a good girl would be expected to eat about five prunes. Any less and she'd marry a tradesman, or a soldier or sailor. (Shock! Horror!) Any more (the greedy child) and she'd end up with a real rascal or someone very down on his luck.

There is, of course, the distinct possibility that the whole thing had less to do with future love and marriage, and more to do with making children eat their lovely prunes (though the same rhyme is sometimes used with the stones of much nicer-tasting cherries too).

## Cowslip balls

Another version of the 'tinker, tailor, soldier, sailor' rhyme accompanies a tradition of children throwing cowslip balls – made from the rounded heads of cowslips, a common wild flower – one to another.

They tossed the ball in time with the rhyme and whoever caught it as it finally fell apart would marry the person who'd just been called out; a rich man if they were lucky!

> Tissty-tossty, tell me true,
> Who am I going to be married to?
> Tinker, tailor, soldier, sailor,
> Rich man, poor man, beggar man, thief.

– Traditional, English

# Dumb Cakes

THE FIRST WRITTEN records of the making of dumb cakes – 'dumb' meaning silent rather than being misused to mean 'stupid' – date back to the 1680s. The cakes weren't supposed to strike one dumb, but had to be made in absolute silence, always by more than one person and usually only by young women.

Dumb cakes were supposed to influence your love life. In other words, the whole preparation and baking of the cake, along with the ritual of what you did with it afterwards, was intended to ensure that the participants could court (and ultimately marry) the people of their choice.

Such cakes often contained unpleasant ingredients, such as soot, and very large quantities of other ingredients, such as salt. Once cooked, people often scratched the initials of loved ones into pieces of the cake, which were then sometimes put under the pillow, perhaps to try to reach their intended 'targets' through their dreams.

Like so many love rituals, dumb cakes were usually made at special times of the year, including Midsummer's Eve and All Hallows' Eve (better known today as Halloween).

# The Hare

IF YOU CHEAT on your lover, beware of the hare!

To the untrained eye, hares look rather like giant bunny rabbits, but have been around in Britain a lot longer than their smaller rivals (imported by the Normans). There's many an old tale of witches turning into hares, and of hares doing the Devil's work, but our interest lies in white-furred hares.

In the West Country, white hares were thought to be the ghosts of girls who took their own lives after being betrayed by their

lovers. They'd come back to haunt them and, in some cases, to try to exact revenge.

One such story tells of a jilted lover who turned into a white hare and frightened her seducer's horse, which then threw him to the ground, breaking his neck.

Hares' hearts were used in spells to turn reluctant lovers into marriage partners or, once again, for revenge. In these instances, it didn't matter what colour the poor hare's fur was.

> *Love is strong as death; jealousy is cruel as the grave.*
>
> From *The Song of Solomon*
> – The Bible, Authorized Version (1611)

# Yarrow

THE NAME 'YARROW' covers a number of wild plants of the same family, with flat clusters of white flower heads. Local names of various varieties include sneezewort and nosebleed . . . and you'll soon see why.

In East Anglia, single girls would pin yarrow to their dresses to try to catch the eye of the boy they were interested in. That was straightforward enough, but on the night of a full moon they also went out barefoot and, with eyes closed, picked a bunch and took it into the house.

If the yarrow was still wet with dew in the

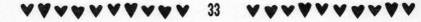

morning, it meant that the girl would soon have a boyfriend.

But now for the really bizarre. In order to find out if a certain boy loved her, the girl would stick a leaf of yarrow up her own nose – yes, you read that correctly – saying:

> *Yarroway, yarroway,*
> *Bear a white blow,*
> *If my love love me,*
> *My nose will bleed now.*

A 'white blow' was the white flower. If her nose bled, then, believe it or not, she thought she was in luck!

In the West Country, there was a tradition of girls picking yarrow at night and putting it under their pillow, chanting:

> *Goodnight, fair yarrow,*
> *Thrice goodnight to thee,*
> *I hope before tomorrow*
> *My true love to see.*

The idea was that they would then dream of the man that they were going to marry. According to some, only yarrow growing over a young man's grave would do the trick.

# Hazelnuts

THE INNOCENT PHRASE 'gathering nuts' used to mean 'making love', as did the phrase 'going nutty' (and I'll bet you thought that simply meant 'going mad'!).

Hazelnuts were often a key ingredient in love divinations. These were rituals usually intended to make a particular person fall in love with you, or to reveal who secretly loved you . . . or, at least, might do one day, if you were lucky.

One such ritual included a boy saying a girl's name before throwing a hazelnut into a bonfire. If the nut burst, 'popping' loudly and flying off through the flames, it meant that the named girl loved, or would come to love, him. (Some believed that if the popping nut actually shot out of the fire and landed in the boy's lap he was guaranteed a successful love match.) For that very reason, in some parts of England, Halloween also became known as Nutcrack Night.

*If you love me, pop and fly.*
*If not, lie and die.*

– Traditional, English

# Sowing the Seed

HEMP USED TO be widely grown for making rope and sacking, and there was a widely held tradition when it came to sowing hemp seed.

As with a number of the rituals discussed in this book, the first written record of this love divination is outlined in *Mother Bunch's Closet*, a rich source of folklore published back in 1685.

According to *Mother Bunch*, the woman sowing the seeds must carry them in her apron, rather than a basket, and say the following chant as she sows:

*Hemp seed I sow,*
*Hemp seed I sow,*
*And he that must be my true love,*
*Come after me and mow.*

After completing – or while completing – the chant for the ninth time, she will see the man she is going to fall in love with and marry . . . or she will hear a bell.

The bell isn't good news, though; hear that instead of seeing a man and, according to some, it meant that the seed-sower would never marry. According to others, it meant that she'd die. The same would happen if she saw a coffin instead of her intended lover!

# The Cuckoo

THE CUCKOO PLAYS a big part in folklore in general and, with its unique approach to parenting (or distinct lack of it by others' standards), small wonder that the cuckoo has a particular place in the lore of love and marriage too.

For those of you not familiar with the cuckoo's behaviour, it lays its single egg in another bird's nest. Once the baby cuckoo is born, it instinctively pushes all other eggs and/or baby birds out of the nest so that the unsuspecting birds feeding it (who have been tricked into believing that they are its parents) are left with a single, very large beak to feed. 'A cuckoo in the nest', therefore, refers to someone who isn't what he purports to be.

In Elizabethan England, the song of the cuckoo was supposed to be mocking husbands whose wives weren't quite what they seemed either: they secretly loved another.

> *Sumer is icumen in –*
> *Lhude sing, cuccu!*
> *Groweth sed, and bloweth med*
> *And springth the wude nu.*
> *Sing, cuccu!*

From 'Cuckoo Song'
– Anonymous (c.1250)

# St Valentine's Day

AS ALL TRUE lovers know, St Valentine's Day is on 14 February of each year and is the day that we send our loved ones cards, flowers and chocolates. Usually the flowers and the chocolates are just for the woman, but (I'm delighted to say) not always. The most romantic of gifts is thought to be a bouquet of a dozen red roses. (See page 47.) Traditionally, such gifts were sent anonymously – in other words, there was nothing but clues to say who they were from – but this is becoming less and less the case.

## It's a date!

The custom of celebrating love and choosing one's sweetheart on 14 February dates back to the fourteenth century in England and France. This was believed to be the date that birds chose their partner in preparation for laying their eggs and rearing their young. The poet Chaucer described the day as being 'when every fowl cometh there to choose his mate'.

The tradition may also have been connected to the ancient Roman festival of Lupercalia, once celebrated on 15 February.

In the early 1400s, John Lydgate (another English poet) actually used the word valentine – though he spelled it 'valantine' – to describe the gift sent *and* the loved one who received it (as in, for example, the saying 'Here's a Valentine for my Valentine').

## Traditions long gone

Past traditions on Valentine's Day included children going from door to door, first thing in the morning, chanting 'Good morrow, Valentine!' and hoping for some cake, fruit or even money for their troubles.

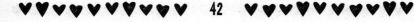

Putting yarrow under one's pillow (see page 34) was also often done on this special day. Another tradition was that the first person you saw on Valentine's Day would be your future husband or wife! Famously, the wife of Samuel Pepys (the seventeenth-century diary writer) covered her eyes with her hands for much of one Valentine's Day, to avoid seeing one of the painters decorating her house at the time. She feared that, if she did, she'd somehow end up marrying the man!

## Letters of love

Today, Valentine's Day is mainly about sending gifts and cards, though a nice candlelit meal never goes amiss. Cards are now very big business, but, even as far back as the middle of the eighteenth century (the 1750s), people were sending each other love letters on Valentine's Day.

By the 1820s, people could buy special Valentine's Day stationery to write them on. By the 1840s, the first printed Valentine's Day cards were on sale. These expensive and ornate cards were often made with lace, silk and even pop-ups and pull-out flaps. Many contained messages of undying love.

Over time, cheaper cards were produced, some of them more jokey and even verging on being plain silly or rude. As a result, by the end of the nineteenth century, the St Valentine's Day tradition had become less and less popular.

## The heart grows fonder

In the 1920s, interest in this special day for lovers was rekindled. When the Second World War started in 1939, many loved ones were separated when people had to go off to fight, to carry out other war duties or to flee from persecution.

Suddenly sending messages of love seemed all the more important.

## Your passion in print

Today, there's a tradition of placing messages of love in newspapers and magazines on St Valentine's Day, ranging from the basic (*'Philip loves Heloise'*) and the soppy (*'Big Cuddles from Mother Morgan to her brave Predator'*) to the downright cryptic (*'LN.UR.4ME.SPLRGG!!!PT.'*), which often will only be understood by the person the message is intended for.

## St Valentine

With all this talk about St Valentine's Day, what about the man it's named after: St Valentine himself? Who was he, and how did he become a saint in the first place? Strangely, the answer is that he was really two people. There were *two* Valentines. They both came to sticky ends and they both became saints!

The first was a Roman pagan priest who gave comfort to persecuted Christians, later becoming a Christian himself. He is said to have performed a miracle by restoring the sight of the blind daughter of the imprisoned Christians' jailer. Despite this good deed he was beaten to death with clubs in about AD 270.

The second Valentine to become a saint was the Bishop of Terni (in what is now Italy), who was also killed for his Christian beliefs. They share 14 February as their saint's day.

*There is a land of pure delight,*
  *Where saints immortal reign.*

From 'A Prospect of Heaven
Makes Death Easy'
– Isaac Watts (1674–1748)

# A Dozen Red Roses

WHAT COULD BE more romantic than being sent a dozen red roses by one's lover – except, perhaps, than receiving a bouquet of eleven and being handed the missing single rose, in person, later in the day?

In medieval times, there was a myth that the first ever roses miraculously appeared in Bethlehem, as a result of the prayers of a pure maiden falsely accused of wrongdoing and about to be burned to death. As she entered the fire, the flaming wood around her turned to red roses.

One of the many titles of Christ's mother,

the Virgin Mary, is 'The Mystical Rose' and many female saints are also associated with the flower. The red rose then came to represent a woman's beauty and to symbolize love.

Today, although given on St Valentine's Day, roses have come to represent *all* forms of love.

What about the significance of there being a dozen? Twelve has always been a special number. Christ had twelve disciples and there are even 'twelve days of Christmas'.

*My luve is like a red, red rose,*
*That's newly sprung in June.*

From 'A Red, Red Rose'
– Robert Burns (1759–1796)

# The Cuckold's Horns

A CUCKOLD IS a man whose wife or girlfriend goes out with *another* man without his knowledge. For hundreds of years, those in the know about such indiscretions have made the sign of two horns behind poor cuckolded men's backs, using their index and little fingers. But how did such a gesture come to symbolize these dirty doings and hanky-panky?

One theory is that many soldiers who went off to fight in the Crusades – leaving their loved ones behind to the temptation of others – had the symbol of the horn on their shields as a part of heraldry. These horns, therefore, came to represent absent men whose wives got up to no good!

## Charlton Horn Fair

One famous story about a cuckold and horns involves a miller catching his wife being kissed by a stranger. The miller is so enraged by what he sees he pulls out his dagger and is about to stab the man when he realizes that he is King John! In return for his life, the King grants the miller various lands, including Charlton, where he permits the miller to hold an annual fair.

Perhaps a little jealous of the miller's new-found riches, the local men make a point of turning up at the fair wearing horns, to represent the cuckold, and even start buying and selling horns at the fair.

If the truth be told, the story probably grew out of the fair, and the real reason for the horns had something to do with the date of the fair: 18 October.

This was St Luke's Day and St Luke was often shown in pictures with a horned ox.

## To their husbands true

According to legend, King Arthur was given a drinking horn by his fairy sister, Morgan Le Fay, called 'The Horn of Fidelity'. The horn had magical properties. Only a woman who was 'to her husband true' could drink from it without spilling a drop. Arthur is said to have given it to King Mark, who tried it out on his queen and a hundred or so ladies in his castle. Only four passed the test . . . which probably tells us more about the original storyteller's low opinion and mistrust of women than anything else!

# Cutting Ties

IT'S A LONG-HELD common belief that you should never give anyone a knife as a present, because it will cut the ties of friendship. The only way around this is to accept a small token – usually a coin – in return. For women wanting to cut links with unwanted lovers, though, the knife is an ideal present. Present it to the man, refusing any gifts in return, and that should get rid of him for once and for all. A knife spun on a table-top, however, may point at your lover-to-be.

# Garters

ONE OF THE few occasions when a person puts on a garter nowadays is when a bride wears one under her wedding dress for good luck. In the past, however, garters were commonly worn by both men and women and could, apparently, be used as a way of finding out who your lover was going to be. Whether you were a man or a woman, the instructions were the same: tie the garter from your left leg to the stocking from your right, reciting a special verse, adding a knot every time you came to a pause.

## THE TRUTH ABOUT LOVE

*This knot I knit,*
*To know the thing,*
*I know not yet,*
*That I may see,*
*The man that shall my husband be,*
*How he goes,*
*And what he wears,*
*And how he does,*
*All days,*
*And all years.*

That night, you would dream of your lover-to-be. What isn't clear is whether you should be *wearing* the garter and stocking when you're doing all this knotting. My guess is, probably not . . .

# Leap Years

EVERY FOUR YEARS, an extra day – 29 February – is added to the calendar so that the calendar year corresponds to the amount of time it takes for the Earth to orbit the Sun. Traditionally, it's only men who can ask women to marry them, and not the other way around, *except* on 29 February. On that day, women can ask men. It's called 'The Ladies' Privilege'. According to some beliefs, a man can't refuse such proposals except by paying a forfeit!

There is a popular misconception that this right is actually enshrined in Scottish

THE TRUTH ABOUT LOVE

Law dating back to the thirteenth century. Fortunately or unfortunately (depending upon how you look at it) this just ain't so.

*Come live with me, and be my love.*

From 'The Passionate Shepherd to His Love'
– Christopher Marlowe (1564–1593)

# Counting Stars

FOR SEVEN NIGHTS in a row, go outside and count seven stars, though not necessarily the same seven. On the eighth day, the first person you shake hands with will become your husband or wife. In a time when handshaking was common courtesy, this could put you in an awkward situation, where you had to go out of your way to avoid shaking certain people's hands. In this day and age, it means that you can track down the person you'd like to marry and shake their hand wholeheartedly!

# The Apple of Your Eye

STAND BEFORE A mirror at midnight on All Hallow's Eve (Halloween) and eat an apple: skin, flesh, core, pips and all. Keep staring into the mirror. Don't glance about and certainly don't turn around. After a while you should see the ghostly reflection of the face of your future husband or wife, as though he or she is looking at you over your shoulder . . .

. . . or so the story goes. Of course, if you stare that long and hard, you may simply start seeing things.

# Your Future in a Bucket?

FILL A BUCKET with fresh spring-water on Midsummer's Day and place it in the middle of a yard. If a girl looks into the bucket and sees nothing more than her own reflection, she will die 'an old maid', unloved and alone. If she sees the reflection of a man's face, this will be the man she will fall in love with and marry.

# Robin Hood and Maid Marian

ONE OF THE most famous romantic couples in English folklore is, of course, the outlaw Robin Hood and his sweetheart, the aristocratic Maid Marian. There are some suggestions that Robin Hood was based on a genuine historical character, two major contenders being Robert, Earl of Huntingdon, and one Robin of Wakefield. Real or not, there were many different stories about him, drawn from different sources. Robin first appears stealing from the rich in rhymes in the 1370s.

There's no mention of his actually giving

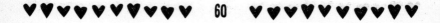

his ill-gotten gains to the poor until the 1500s, which is about the time that Maid Marian turns up in the stories. As for Robin once being a nobleman before becoming an outlaw, that doesn't appear in writing until 1569.

What adds to the confusion is that the names Robin and Marion (with an 'o') have been the stock names for country lovers with the French since the thirteenth century (in much the same way that the English use Tom, Dick and Harry to describe any Tom, Dick or Harry!).

Then, to make things even more complicated, there was an Elizabethan character called Marian, often represented by a man dressed in women's clothing, who fooled around with another man dressed as the Fool. No one's quite sure which Marian/Marion came first and influenced the others!

## Other famous lovers

No list of lovers would be complete without the following, some real and some imagined:

CASANOVA: a real person (1725–1798) who wrote about his love life, and who gives his name to a man with many lovers (as in 'he's a bit of a Casanova').

ROMEO AND JULIET: Shakespeare's star-crossed lovers (from feuding families) who both end up dead at their own hands.

SALUZZO AND GRISELDA: He is a marquis, and she a beautiful poor girl. They marry but he puts her through many tests to prove her devotion and patience. The story was first told in the mid-fourteenth century.

ABELARD AND HÉLOÏSE: French twelfth-century tutor and pupil who secretly marry then are forced to separate; he entering a monastery and she becoming a nun. They are buried side by side.

GUINEVERE AND LANCELOT: King Arthur's queen and his finest knight who, according to legend, fall madly in love, ultimately leading to the end of Camelot and the Knights of the Round Table.

# Midsummer Men

ANOTHER NAME FOR orpine, a plant with purply-white flowers, is Midsummer Men, and it's at the centre of one of the many 'love divination' rituals which are supposed to be carried out on Midsummer's Eve. On this particular day, in one version of the custom, a man and a woman (wanting to find out whether they'll make a good couple) both pick slips of orpine. The flowers are then stuck in the ground facing each other and the couple wait for them to droop.

The more the flowers bend *towards* each other – like lovers wanting to be close to

each other – the more compatible the man and woman are said to be. If most of the orpine slips bend away from each other, though, the relationship is supposed to be doomed before it's even started.

A variation on the ritual has the plants being pulled up (rather than plucked) and replanted in pairs by different couples. If one or both of the plants in a pair soon shrivels up and dies, then that couple's relationship is expected to fail too.

Unlike similar rituals which petered out a long, long time ago, the 'Midsummer Men' custom – which was certainly widespread in the early seventeenth century – was still very popular right into the twentieth century.

Orpine also goes by the name of 'livelong' in Britain and 'live-forever' in the US. Perhaps that should be 'lovelong'.

# Redheads

IN ENGLAND, IT used to be a distinct disadvantage in the love-and-marriage stakes if you were a redhead. People with red hair were supposed to suffer from everything from bad behaviour to bad breath! They were even said to smell like foxes (which are similarly red) and be nothing but trouble.

In medieval times, many believed that Cain, who killed Abel (in the Old Testament), and Judas, who betrayed Christ (in the New Testament), were both redheads. But how on earth did such a bad reputation befall people with red hair?

Obviously if someone has a fiery temper and flaming red hair then a superficial connection might be made between the two, but the truth is probably something far more obvious.

The English and the Scots may share an island, but they have been traditional enemies for much of history . . . and many Scottish people are redheaded. Other traditional enemies of the English include the Vikings, famous for their raping, pillaging and big red beards! An English person with red hair was, therefore, probably originally suspected of being descended from the Enemy with a capital 'E'!

All was not lost though. There were some who thought that redheads were particularly passionate lovers.

# A Lady's Favour

IN DAYS OF old, when knights were bold, they'd often wear a lady's favour – a coloured scarf tied around the wrist, for example – to show that they were competing in a joust or at a tournament in the name of that particular lady. This was just one aspect of courtly love in the Age of Chivalry. Chivalry was a code of conduct (differing from country to country and time to time) by which a good, true knight was supposed to live, covering all aspects of his behaviour from the battlefield to home life.

A variation on the lady's favour was the

coloured favours – often ribbons – worn by men at certain country festivals and revels, pinned in place by their women and clearly stating 'He's mine'! Today, most ribbons pinned to lapels are a statement about supporting a cause, not about who belongs to whom.

*Whenever you are confronted with an opponent, conquer him with love.*

– Mahatma Gandhi (1869–1948)

# Puppy Love

IN THE SAME way that 'cupboard love' is
not a love *of* cupboards, *for* cupboards or
even *in* cupboards, puppy love is not the love
between two young dogs. No. Puppy love is a
slightly derogatory term for the love between
two young people. It suggests that the so-
called love is not the real thing and will be
grown out of. It's a temporary infatuation.
It's less commonly known as calf love (as in
a young cow, as opposed to a leg calf).

Child singing sensation Donny Osmond
had a huge hit with the song 'Puppy Love'
in 1972.

And, for those of you who don't know, cupboard love is love inspired by a greedy motive (e.g. a pet loving you in return for food from the cupboard).

*Love keeps the cold out better than a cloak.*

From *The Spanish Student*
– Henry Wadsworth Longfellow
(1807–1882)

# Poetry and Song

ONE OF THE few occasions when just about everybody turns their hand to having a go at writing verse – perhaps 'poetry' would be too grand a term for it – is when they're in love. (Even if it's only a few lines scribbled on the back of an old envelope, which is then hurriedly thrown away.) Sometimes, only poetry – or, perhaps, song – will do the trick.

## The immortal Bard

Perhaps the most famous writer of love poetry in the English language is William

Shakespeare, who wrote a series of love sonnets. (A sonnet is a poem of fourteen lines, following a series of strict rules, including rhyming scheme.) The best-known of these is probably the one beginning, *'Shall I compare thee to a summer's day?'*. Other great love poets include John Donne (who, as a 'metaphysical poet', was concerned with the big issues of the human condition, particularly love and death) and Lord Byron (who was as famous for his love affairs as his poetry!).

## The Rubáiyát of Omar Khayyám

The love poetry of the twelfth-century Persian poet Omar Khayyám became famous in the English-speaking world when a translation of his anthology or *Rubáiyát*, by Edward FitzGerald, was published in 1859.

## Love songs

Today, there are many contemporary poets still writing of love but, with the advent of recorded music and video, it is the love

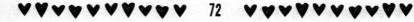

*song*, rather than love poem, which has taken over the world. Of all the songs in all the world, by far the most are about one subject: LOVE.

> *Love made me poet*
> *And this I writ;*
> *My heart did do it,*
> *And not my wit.*

From an epitaph on her husband's tomb
– Lady Elizabeth Tanfield (c.1565–1628)

# The Power of Numbers

NUMEROLOGY IS THE study of numbers – say, for example, the figures in your date of birth – and their supposed influence on human lives. Numerology is treated as a 'science' by some people, who take it very seriously, and as a bit of fun by others. One of the biggest areas of numerology deals with, you guessed it, LOVE. More often than not, numerology deals with the numbers in dates as single digits rather than the whole number. For example, the year 1961 would be treated as the numbers 1,9,6 and 1.

To someone looking for love, even the most unlikely everyday objects can hold 'clues'. In the 1950s, Peter and Iona Opie, the famous collectors of folklore, found that numerology even extended to the numbers on bus tickets. Using various complicated calculations, letter-for-number substitutions and other playground hocus-pocus, children claimed to be able to determine the initials of the one they would fall in love with and eventually marry, and even the date of the wedding . . . all from the digits on a ticket!

*I have often admired the mystical way of Pythagoras, and the secret magic of numbers.*

From *Religio Medici*
– Sir Thomas Browne (1605–1682)

# Narcissus

IF SOMEONE SHOWS an unhealthy admiration for himself – especially if he spends an inordinate amount of time preening himself in front of the mirror – then he could be described as being narcissistic. (This applies to women too.)

The word 'narcissism' comes from the ancient Greek legend of the beautiful boy Narcissus, who fell in love with his own reflection. What's slightly misleading is that Narcissus had no idea that he was looking at himself . . . unlike the narcissists named after him!

# Astrology

ASTROLOGISTS BELIEVE – OR claim to believe – that the movement and position of planets have control over people's lives; that by creating a chart based on the position of these celestial bodies on the exact day and time of a person's birth, it is possible to make accurate predictions about that person's future, including their love life. Mapped out in a special circle called an ecliptic, this is a personal horoscope.

More general horoscopes, based simply on the day and month of birth (and not the year) can be found in many newspapers and magazines. You simply look under your sun sign – often known as a star sign or sign of the zodiac – to see what's supposed to be in store for you. Such predictions are usually suitably vague. Your star sign depends upon when you were born:

| | |
|---|---|
| 20 Jan–18 Feb | *Aquarius* the water carrier |
| 19 Feb–20 Mar | *Pisces* the fish |
| 21 Mar–19 Apr | *Aries* the ram |
| 20 Apr–20 May | *Taurus* the bull |
| 21 May–21 Jun | *Gemini* the heavenly twins |
| 22 Jun–22 Jul | *Cancer* the crab |
| 23 July–22 Aug | *Leo* the lion |
| 23 Aug–22 Sep | *Virgo* the maiden |
| 23 Sep–23 Oct | *Libra* the weighing scales |
| 24 Oct–21 Nov | *Scorpio* the scorpion |
| 22 Nov–21 Dec | *Sagittarius* the archer |
| 22 Dec–19 Jan | *Capricorn* the goat |

# She Loves Me . . .

ONE OF THE most common 'tests' to see whether someone loves you is to pull the petals off a flower. As you pull the first petal, you say: 'S/he loves me . . .' As you pull the second, you say: 'S/he loves me not . . .' The third: 'S/he loves me . . .' and so on, until you reach the final petal. This is the one which matters. If it's a 'S/he loves me' petal, you're in luck. (Here's a good – if obvious – tip: be sure to choose a flower with an odd number of petals!) This love divination is still popular today as a bit of fun. The daisy is the flower traditionally used for this ritual because it is known as the 'flower of Venus'.

Different flowers have different meanings (and to make things more complicated some single flowers have many different meanings). Here are just a few simple examples, if you want to 'say it with flowers':

| FLOWER: | MEANS: |
| --- | --- |
| Buttercup | Beauty |
| Heather | Friendship |
| Violet | First love |
| Red carnation | Longing to meet |
| Pink carnation | A woman's love |
| Orange blossom | Pure love |
| Mallow | Devotion |
| Love-lies-bleeding | Heartbreak |
| Red rose | Passionate love |
| Rosemary | Fond memories of a departed loved one |

# Dreams

FOR THOUSANDS OF years, it's been a commonly held belief that dreams may predict the future or contain nuggets of vital information. One area of particular interest has always been the significance of dreams in predicting who you might fall in love with and whether that love will run smooth.

Numerous books have been written on the subject, allocating particular meanings to particular objects and events. Some interpretations seem obvious, some unlikely, some downright perverse!

Some common beliefs include:

| DREAMING OF: | MEANS: |
|---|---|
| A dove in flight | Good news on its way |
| A tree falling | A relationship is ending |
| Clear water | Emotional happiness |
| Murky water | Emotional confusion |
| Stormy water/waves | Emotional trouble ahead |
| Small birds | Joy |
| A coal fire | Happiness in the home |
| A red rose | The deepest love |
| Being given a ring | Marriage |
| Losing a ring | Doubts about a relationship |
| Breaking a ring | A relationship will break up |
| A fairy | A wish will come true |
| An angel | Spiritual happiness |

Sigmund Freud, the founder of psycho-analysis, believed that we each have an 'unconscious mind': the part of our brain which has a big effect on why we do things

without us realizing why we do them. Dreams, he reasoned, were dramas played out in the unconscious mind. If one's dreams could be understood – psychoanalysed – then that would help us understand why people behave as they do without an obvious reason.

*The interpretation of dreams is the royal road to a knowledge of the unconscious activities of the mind.*

From *The Interpretation of Dreams*
– Sigmund Freud (1856–1939)

*Thus I have thee, as a dream doth flatter,*
*In sleep a king but, waking, no such matter.*

From Sonnet 87
– William Shakespeare (1564–1616)

# Apple Peel

CAN YOU CUT the peel off an apple in one whole piece? You can? Then you're well on the way to discovering who you'll end up marrying. The trick with the peeling part is to cut it in a spiral. The trick with the discovering-who-you'll-end-up-marrying part is to throw the whole piece of apple peel over your right shoulder. When it lands, it should form the initials – in one piece or more – of the person you're going to marry. Good luck.

# Apple Peel

CAN YOU CUT the peel of an apple in one whole piece? You can't? Then you're well on the way to discovering why you'll end up marrying. The trick with the peeling part is to cut it in a spiral. The trick with the fortune-telling who-you-at-end-up-marrying part is to throw the whole piece of apple peel over your right shoulder. When it lands, it should form the initials — in one piece or other — of the person you're going to marry.

# INDEX